The New England
EXPERIENCE

Love

Sam
&
Haley

Other Books by Don Bousquet

BEWARE OF THE QUAHOG

THE QUAHOG WALKS AMONG US

I BRAKE FOR QUAHOGS

The New England EXPERIENCE

Cartoons from the pages of *YANKEE* Magazine

By Don Bousquet

YANKEE BOOKS

A division of
Yankee Publishing Incorporated
Dublin, New Hampshire

Designed by Margo Letourneau

Most of the cartoons in this collection
have previously been published in *Yankee* Magazine.

Yankee Publishing Incorporated
Dublin, New Hampshire 03444

First Edition
Third Printing, 1987
Copyright 1987 by Yankee Publishing Incorporated

Library of Congress Catalogue Card Number: 86-51017

ISBN: 0-89909-123-7

The Making of a Cartoonist

Few people know early in life that they will become cartoonists. Don Bousquet was not one of the exceptions. This is reassuring, especially to those of us who don't know what we plan to do if we ever grow up. Don began his journey toward the world of humor and cartoons innocently enough: he was born in Rhode Island. ("Keep your smart remarks to yourself.") The irony was that, although he came from 100% Irish stock and was born on St. Patrick's Day, his surname suggests a French heritage. Life quickly filled with more confusion.

None of Don's grade-school teachers can recall that he exhibited any remarkable talent as a caricaturist during his formative years, although he did show an inclination toward art. It must have been events later in his life that turned him to his current trade. Perhaps it was the Navy, in which Don enlisted in 1966. (Well, actually he was drafted, but he *did* exercise his right to choose his preferred branch of the service.) The Navy offered him the opportunity to attend drafting school, but somewhere between enlistment and induction that option disappeared and Don became a Navy photographer. Most likely this was the inadvertent turning point in his career. Once someone finds ironic humor in day-to-day life, it is nearly impossible not to see it everywhere. This was the continuing lesson that Don learned in his life after the Navy.

Few jobs back in Rhode Island required the skills of a former Navy photographer, so Don signed on with the world-famous Pinkerton Detective Agency. His first assignment was to work undercover in a sanitary napkin factory. Yes, he did solve the case (discovering that some of the plant's output was making its way to North Vietnam as field bandages), but in the process he decided that the glamorous world of the private eye was not to be his. College at this point looked like a good option.

It was at the University of Rhode Island that Don finally took his first, and only, introductory art course — Art 101. He got a C. Clearly he was on the right track, but his experience in the Navy had taught him to look ahead to possible future employment after graduation, and he questioned the value of an art degree in the Rhode Island job market. Fortunately he didn't have to go beyond the front of the course catalog to find his chosen field. Anthropology had a nice, useful ring to it. In retrospect, Don defends his choice with perfect logic. "After all," he says, "what does a cartoonist do but observe people and their culture? Sounds a lot like anthropology to me." He went to college year-round, taking maximum course loads. In only two and a half years he graduated, trained and ready to study any culture, great or small.

Once again, Don was a helpless victim of the home state he loves so much. As advanced as society was in the Rhode Island of the early 1970s, there was no clear mandate for a native anthropologist to begin work. Don did the next best thing: he found a job. Working at a vocational placement agency, Don learned to pick his way through the labyrinthine halls of state bureaucracy. His appreciation of large institutions stems from this period and is a theme that appears frequently in Don's early cartoons.

Meanwhile, Don's wife, Laura, had harvested her master's degree and landed a teaching job in Exeter–West Greenwich. Life began to settle in for the long haul at the Bousquet household, and with it a certain measure of comfort.

Unfortunately, Don had an itch. Maybe it came from doodling on notepads while he was solving the jigsaw puzzles of state regulations on the phone. Maybe it was all the time he spent each day commuting to Providence from their home in Narragansett. Whatever the reason, Don became ever more certain that he would become a cartoonist. After six years on the job his resolution was strong and the time seemed right.

The very evening that Don arrived home to tell his wife that he had made the break — quit his good-paying job to become a cartoonist, without a single published cartoon to his credit — Laura arrived home with her own exciting news: "Honey, guess what? We're going to have a baby!" Recalling that evening, and the subsequent four and a half months it took to sell his first cartoon, Don waxes philosophical: "Oh, no question, the impending arrival of Nathan Patrick helped me appreciate the importance of *selling* cartoons, as opposed to just *being* a cartoonist."

By cartoonist's standards, Don has achieved a fair measure of success. Despite his initial belief that the only place in which he should publish his work was *The New Yorker*, Don did a very smart thing: he developed a local market. He first attracted a loyal following through his early appearances in *The Providence Journal*, and his first three books all draw their humor from Rhode Island and its immediate environs. Since 1982, Don has captured all of "The New England Experience" (and with it a nationwide audience) in the pages of *Yankee* Magazine.

So read on and enjoy. There is much to laugh at in this little book and even a little to learn. After all, the author is an anthropologist who draws funny.

– John Pierce
Managing Editor
Yankee *Magazine*

REGISTRY
OF
MOTOR VEHICLES

DON BOUSQUET

INDIANA JONES AND THE TEMPLE OF DOOM

" HE HOVERS PRETTY GOOD FOR A MONGREL... YOU'RE GOING TO HAVE TO DO SOMETHING ABOUT THAT SHEDDING PROBLEM THOUGH. "

"HE FOLLOWED ME HOME. CAN I KEEP HIM MA?? CAN I?!"

GOVERNOR'S MANSION, MAINE

OFF-SEASON FOLIAGE TOURISTS

"BELIEVE IT OR NOT THE FURNACE DIDN'T COME ON ONCE THIS WINTER."

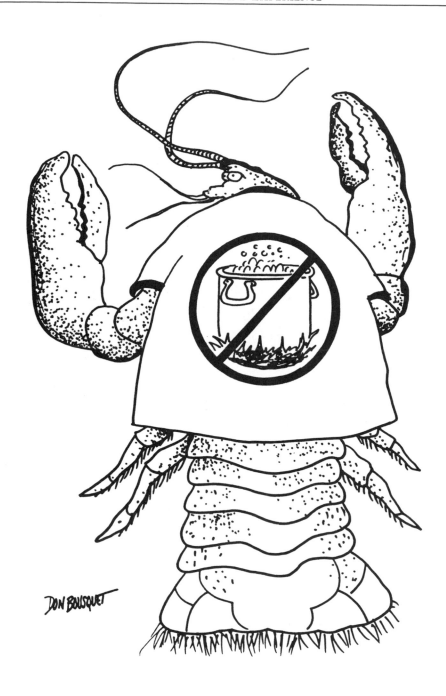

DAY 117 — SUDDENLY I REALIZED
I'D MISSED FOLIAGE SEASON...

" OOOOOOO! WE CAUGHT ONE! THERE'S ONE IN THERE!! I'M NOT REACHING IN THERE, NO WAY!!! "

" I'M GOING TO CALL IT AN APPARENT SUICIDE... "

"THIS MONTH'S 'HOUSE FOR SALE' IS A CONVERTED BOWLING ALLEY IN ORONO."

" ...THEN IN JANUARY OF FIFTY-FIVE THE BLOCK CRACKED AND SHE SEIZED UP PRETTY GOOD. YOUR FATHER SAID HE WAS GOING DOWN TO THE KAISER DEALER IN MONTPELIER FOR PARTS. THAT WAS THE LAST I SEEN OF YOUR FATHER. "

"WELL, MOTHER; THE MILLINOCKET 'UNION LEADER' CAUTIONS US TO EXPECT A COLDER THAN USUAL WINTER."

CAPTAIN JAMES T. KIRK OF THE LOBSTER BOAT...

"THE 'SURF' IS A SUMPTUOUS SERVING OF TENDER, BAKED, STUFFED, JUMBO SHRIMP AN' THE 'TURF' IS A GENEROUS CLUMP OF SOD WITH SOME SORT OF LONG, GREEN SHOOTS STICKING UP OUT OF IT."

GRADUATE OF A NON-ACCREDITED HIGH SCHOOL

NORM NOW RENTS-TO-OWN AT THE
MEN'S HAIRPIECE AND DENTURE CENTER
OF WORCESTER — AND THE BEST PART
IS, ALL HIS FRIENDS THINK HE'S LOSING
WEIGHT!

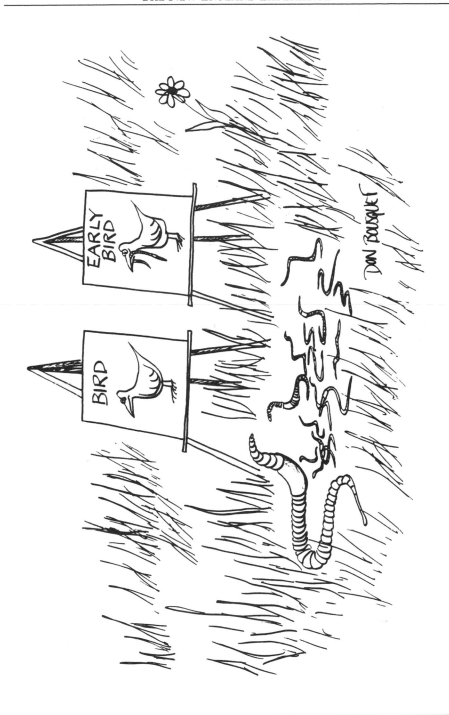

" WHO'S GOT THE EXTRA LARGE
PIZZA WITH EVERYTHING ?! "

THERE WAS AN OLD WOMAN WHO LIVED IN A (PASSIVE SOLAR) SHOE...

"WHEN YOU GET TO MY CHIMNEY YOU'RE GOING TO BE CONFRONTED BY AN AIR-TIGHT FIRE-PLACE INSERT WITH A THREE-STAGE BLOWER MANIFOLD AND A CATALYTIC COMBUSTOR... I'LL LEAVE THE BACK DOOR AJAR."

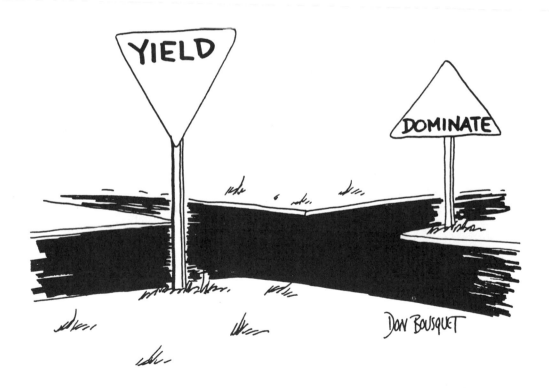

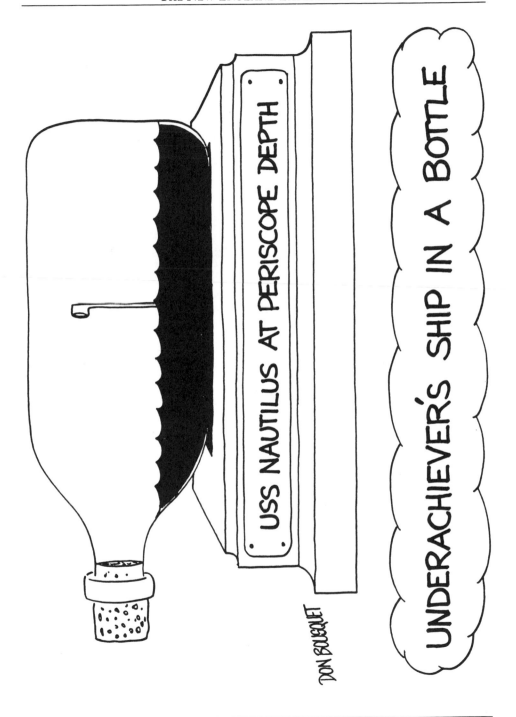

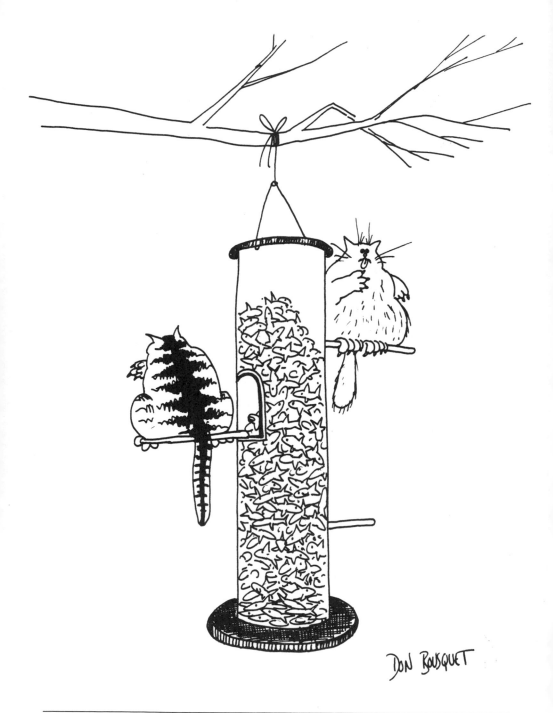

DON BOUSQUET

" I'VE TRIED THEM ALL, YOUNG MAN —
ACTIVE AND PASSIVE SOLAR, COAL, OIL,
KEROSENE AND WOOD BURNERS. BUT WHEN
WINTER ARRIVES YOU JUST CAN'T BEAT
FLYING YOUR FANNY DOWN TO FORT
LAUDERDALE. "

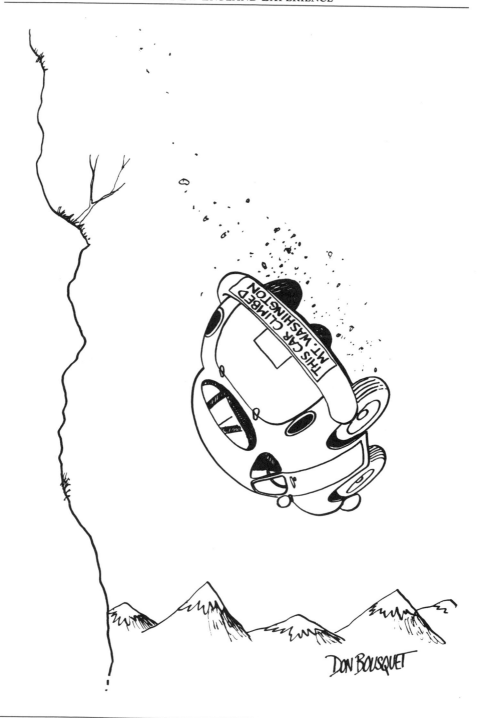

" IT MUST BE A BLEAK SORT OF LIFE —
HOLED UP IN THERE WITH ONLY OCCASIONAL
REFILLINGS OF OUR FEEDER TO RELIEVE
THE TEDIUM..."

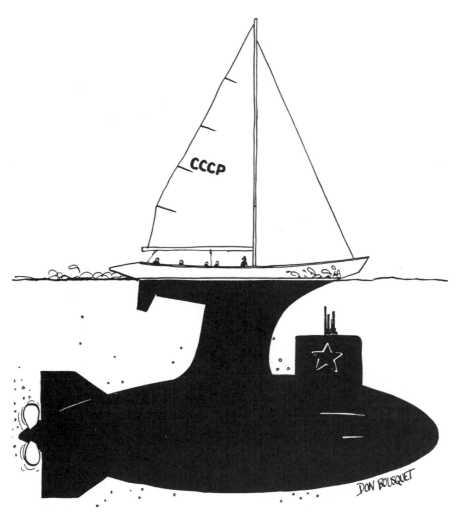

YET ANOTHER CONTENDER PREPARES A SECRET KEEL-
EQUIPPED TWELVE-METER YACHT FOR THE NEXT ROUND
OF AMERICA'S CUP RACES AT PERTH.

JOHN HOUSEMAN BREAK DANCING
FOR SMITH - BARNEY.

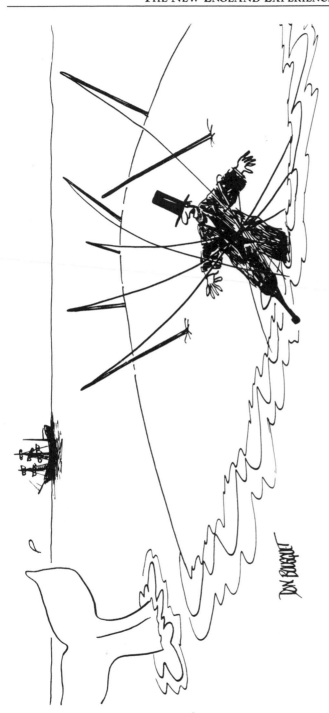

"HOLD MY CALLS!"

"KITTERY AIN'T SUCH A BAD TOWN.
IT'S JUST THAT NOTHING EVER SEEMS
TO HAPPEN HERE..."

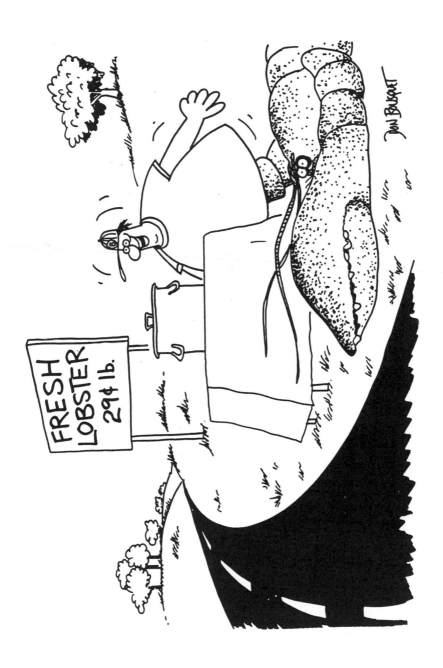

THE ORIGIN
OF
QUEEN ANNE STYLE
FURNITURE

TEENAGE MR. SPOCK

" I DUNNO, TEACH ... MAYBE IF I GRADUATE I'LL LAND A GIG WITH THE FEDERATION ... "

BACK IN THE DAYS BEFORE INDOOR PLUMBING A BREEZEWAY WOULD HAVE BEEN A REAL CONVENIENCE.

RHODE ISLAND — WHERE EVEN
TEENAGERS CLING TO TRADITIONAL
VALUES.

"LET'S JUST STOP AND THINK FOR A MINUTE ... WE MUST BE DOING SOMETHING WRONG ... "

"GREETINGS! I REPRESENT A WOOD-BURNING RACE FROM A DISTANT GALAXY AND I CAN'T TELL YOU HOW MUCH WE LOVE MAINE!"

WHAT FLAMINGOS HAVE ON THEIR
LAWNS...

THEY COULD HAVE SAVED A LOT OF MONEY
VINYL SIDING THE STATUE OF LIBERTY.

" WELL, THE SQUIRRELS HAVE GONE BUT
WE MAY HAVE ANOTHER PROBLEM... "

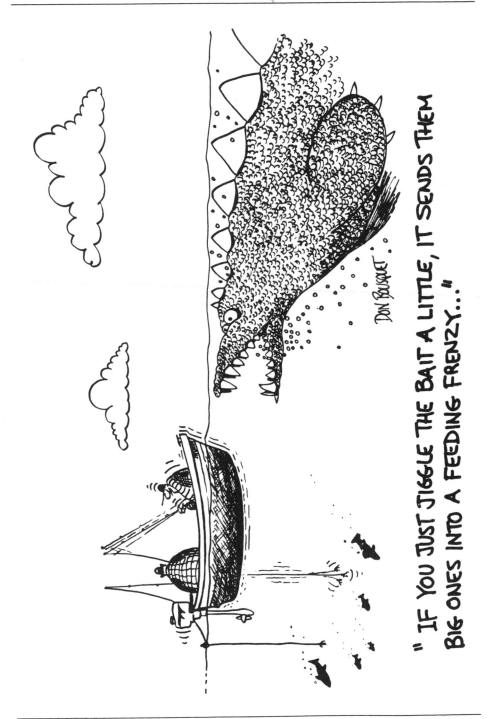

"IF YOU JUST JIGGLE THE BAIT A LITTLE, IT SENDS THEM BIG ONES INTO A FEEDING FRENZY..."

" HELLO? MR. HENDERSON? ERNEST WON'T BE IN TODAY — THE NEW <u>YANKEE</u> JUST ARRIVED. "

"GRAN'PA, I'M WORKING ON A CLASS
PROJECT AT SCHOOL AND I NEED TO
KNOW HOW LONG YOU'VE BEEN CHICKEN
FARMING HERE IN WOODSTOCK..."

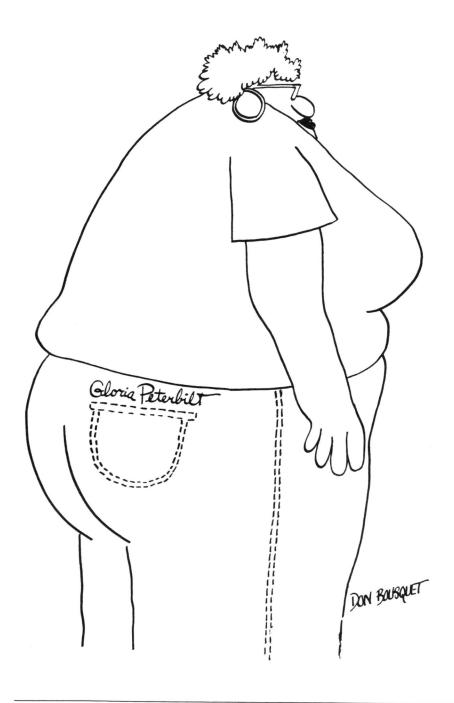

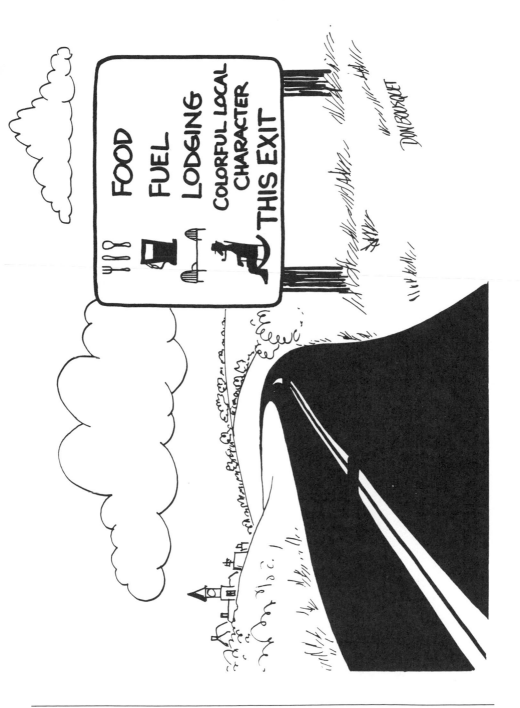

ONE OF THE PERILS
OF WATER SKIING ON
LAKE CHAMPLAIN

BUDGET CAT SCAN

" JUST LEAN OVER THE SIDE AND SCOOP HIM IN — AND FOR GOD'S SAKE BE CAREFUL — SOMETIMES THE LITTLE DEVILS HAVE THOSE POINTY LITTLE SPINES ON TOP OF THEIR..."

DON BOUSQUET

" ...CHOWDA ... CHOWDA... "

" MUST BE A PRIVATE BEACH . "

VALIANT YET SELDOM REMEMBERED
UNION SOLDIER, GENERAL ROBERT E.
LIEBOWITZ, "THE FIGHTING RABBI"

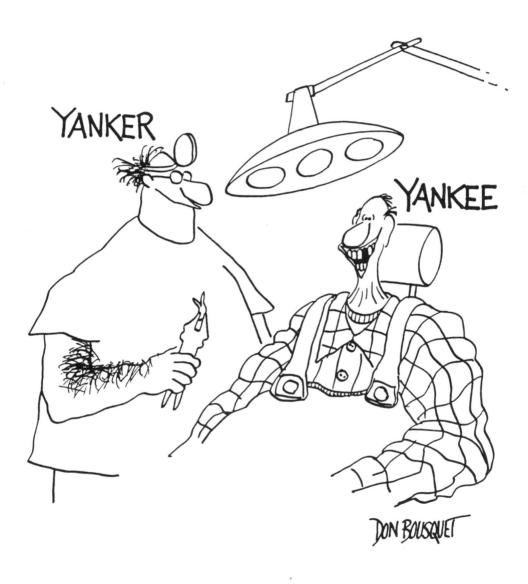

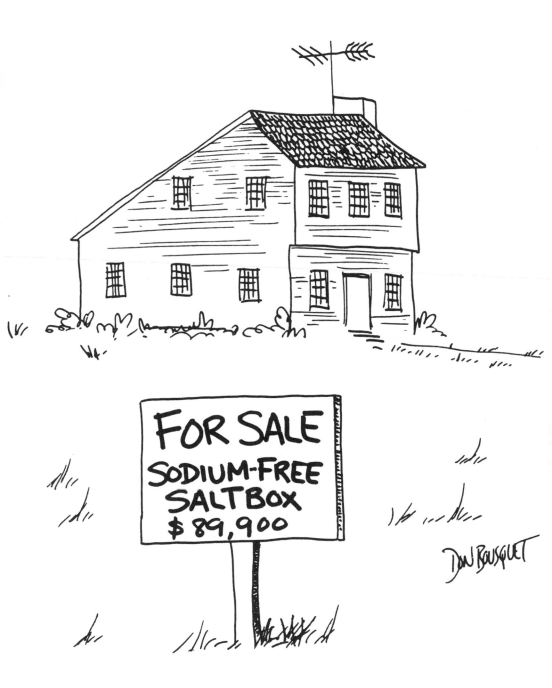

" MY GRANPA SAYS WHEN YOU SEE THEM ALL
LYING DOWN IT'S GOING TO RAIN. "

AND NOW...

COUNTERFEIT TODDLERS' CLOTHES

"WE USED TO LIVE IN PAWTUCKET BUT MY DAD WANTED TO WAKE UP IN A CITY THAT DOESN'T SLEEP. SO WE MOVED TO WORCESTER."

EIGHTH RUNNER UP,
ELVIS PRESLEY LOOK-ALIKE CONTEST

JELLYFISH

PEANUTBUTTERFISH

DON BOUSQUET

"REMIND ME TO FINE-TUNE THE TENSION ADJUSTMENT ON UNCLE ROY'S UP-AN'-AT-'EM ROCKER..."

TRAINING ROCKER
FOR THE NEWLY RETIRED

About the Author

D on Bousquet was born in Pawtucket, Rhode Island, on St. Patrick's Day, 1948. He was raised in Richmond, Rhode Island, and graduated from Chariho High School. Before attending the University of Rhode Island, where he majored in anthropology, Don served in the Navy as a photographer and worked as a private investigator for the Pinkerton Detective Agency.

His cartoons regularly appear in *The Narragansett Times, The Standard-Times, The Providence Journal, Yankee* Magazine, and *The Old Farmer's Almanac.* Don lives in Narragansett, Rhode Island, with his wife, Laura, and his two sons, Nathan and Michael. His hobbies include antique cars, boating, and sailplanes.

Photograph by Sallie W. Latimer